THE

SEL

ESSENTIAL POETS SERIES 130

Canada Council for the Arts Conseil des Arts du Canada

ONTARIO ARTS COUNCIL
CONSEIL DES ARTS DE L'ONTARIO

Guernica Editions Inc. acknowledges the support of
The Canada Council for the Arts.
Guernica Editions Inc. acknowledges the support of
the Ontario Arts Council.

LOUISE DUPRÉ

THE BLUENESS OF LIGHT

SELECTED POEMS: 1988-2002

TRANSLATED BY ANTONIO D'ALFONSO

GUERNICA
TORONTO · BUFFALO · CHICAGO · LANCASTER (U.K.)
2005

Antonio D'Alfonso, editor
Guernica Editions Inc.
P.O. Box 117, Station P, Toronto (ON), Canada M5S 2S6
2250 Military Road, Tonawanda, N.Y. 14150-6000 U.S.A.

Distributors:
University of Toronto Press Distribution,
5201 Dufferin Street, Toronto (ON), Canada M3H 5T8

Gazelle Book Services, White Cross Mills, High Town,
Lancaster LA1 1XS U.K.

Independent Publishers Group,
814 N. Franklin Street, Chicago, Il. 60610 U.S.A.

First edition.
Printed in Canada.

Legal Deposit – Third Quarter
National Library of Canada
Library of Congress Catalog Card Number: 2003105515

National Library of Canada Cataloguing in Publication
Dupré, Louise
The blueness of the light : selected poems 1988-2002 /
Louise Dupré ; translated by Antonio D'Alfonso.
(Essential poets series ; 130)
ISBN 1-55071-203-9
1. Dupré, Louise. Translations into English.
I. D'Alfonso, Antonio. II. Title. III. Series.
PS8557.U66B58 2004 C841'.54 C2003-907510-9

CONTENTS

ACKNOWLEDGEMENTS

Louise Dupré made this selection from the works she has published.

When asked if "Notes on Survival" could close the volume, Louise Dupré hinted that it would symbolically put an end to the medical ordeal her partner had been suffering for a year.

Man and woman emerge from the night and wager everything they have in order to assure their own survival. Intransigence of this kind is tolerable only if tempered by tenderness, and we find plenty of gentleness in these pages.

All my thanks to Louise Dupré for her astute reading. A warm thank you to Elana Wolff for offering her editorial suggestions.

The poems were chosen from *Voice Over:* "Voix off," in *Bonheur,* Montréal: Éditions du Noroît, 1988; *A Hole of Silence:* "Trou de silence," in *Noir déjà,* Montreal: Éditions du Noroît, 1993; *Without a Witness:* "Sans témoin," *Les écrits,* No. 90, August 1997; *So Close:* in *Tout près*, Montréal: Éditions du Noroît, 1998; *Notes on Survival:* "Carnets de la survie, "*Liberté,* No. 258, Vol. 44, No. 4, November 2002.

VOICE OVER

1988

1

When I wake up at night I'm afraid you will ask me who I am. The heart's gone crazy. I sniff for your scent. Surfaces. I stop moving. I must not move. I wait for the images to slowly fade away. When I'm lying beside you, I want to be a woman without history. I stretch out my hands to the morning light and compose goodness, no matter how miserable the planets are. I believe that nothing can happen to our bodies if they embrace the world and the concreteness of objects: the first cup of coffee, my hands in the humid crassula earth, my fingers graze the curtain, lightness of lace against my cheek. You are deep asleep, unaware of me. This is how I want you. Sleeping.

2

You are sleeping. Sound asleep. Smiling. What dreams pull you away from terror? In vain I try to gather myself. Dawn spits me up. Breathless. I stand in front of a castle in ruins, its turrets and dungeons shifting on the beach I walk to, feeling alive. Some images can kill you. Lose me in your sleep. I pull up the bedsheet. Outside the window, I can almost touch the fresh air in our garden. The world is falling in order. Movement starts where night left it. My heart is a hollow muscle. Again. I am a woman who contains in her unbound greatness all of the earth's tremors.

3

I am the woman of the morning light. My vibrancy is frail in the garden, as my fingers, deep in the soil, awaken the glory of the world. But she is blind to this. Her stomach is empty. She needs to grow roots in the ground of this scene. You do not notice how this woman manages the longevity of chaos. Gently the wind rocks her, lulls her. Beauty rises from the light. This is a joyous woman ignorant of the cruel night that snatches my name from me. Does she think of me when the ram sneers at my skin? Veiled by a cloud, I snug myself against your back and breathe in your breath. You are asleep, you are asleep, and calm. You are unaware that a mouth has opened wide over my life.

4

In the morning I am the woman who stretches like a cat, body-silence in the vegetation and dew. She is resting, she is resting, a fossil soul howling under the moon, alive with summer night. She tames dirt and all matter. Neutral. Merciless to suffering and beautiful indiffercnce that gradually dims her vision. Does she hear the distant rumour – car horns and other melodies –as truth grabs her with declawed fingers in the quivering water of an embrace?

5

Morning desperately whispers hello. How to explain this to you? Each morning I rise alive from my own ruin and glue happiness back together again. I'm getting used to the heat and don't think of hell. I know you are there, beside me, breathing without pain, in our bedroom, as I care for our plants. Vegetation tears apart our human envelope. Breathing becomes a gift, a space waiting to be filled. We discover in words the whitish paste and weight of sacrifice.

6

It is while you are asleep that I belong to you. I look at you through the window. You are sound asleep. I watch over your tired muscles. In the empty garden, I surrender to dizziness, the noise in the hollow of the ear, a language freed of its familiar ghosts. The world wavers. I do not speak. Confessing would be futile. Perhaps there exists a reality that runs against fate, chance turned inside out to become plenitude. The present and all its hand-me-downs slip into the swarming summer. Everywhere, the sounds of pain, the sounds of joy.

7

Beneath these images, a creature feels a sorrow that no outcry can save. Listen to me in your sleep. Listen. Joy is not the opposite of melancholy; it is a wall of light. Every morning, I step on what seems a freshly painted hardwood foor. To become one with the bedsheet is to say no to dawn, no to ecstasy, no to animated curves. Waking up every morning is a compromise. The earth in the garden is humid, fingers fashion new galaxies, the wedding band is soiled. I go blind.

8

And to say that we almost did not meet. We could have crossed one another's path, each walking at the edges of our lives, each wearing a wedding band. Loving is a stroke of luck, a dice that rolls towards the four-leaf clover over which we are bent, one finding the other, a miracle. Between us a common voice. Tomorrow rings, tomorrow, tomorrow is significant. We overthrow our kingdoms and find a soul, a thing, a tide, sweet-smelling drops of sweat at our lips. We use Latin words to describe fidelity.

9

Do you see legs dangling over the edge? Ghosts sleep under my eyelids. Dreams are crowded with people, colors, chipped plaster debris. We'll never get used to such ruins. The road is empty, without passerby or swallow. The bedsheet is hurting, even if it is imbued with the sweetness of love. The bedsheet screams. I position my feet on the trembling tightrope. No one is looking at me. No one will catch me if I fall. Where are you? You join me, face the facts. Nothing is ever shared in sleep.

10

You are asleep. Between your teeth, a landscape of orchids and giant trees. Reality, as you know, no matter how small, can still be cut to smaller rectangular pieces. The ground has no sense of its curves. Curls become entangled. The universe is asunder, you are asleep, unaware that it is about to explode. At dawn a woman is born. She gathers the stones of the universe and forgets. Twilight again. Tomorrow she starts all over again. The garden is an extension of the bedroom. The ambiguous horizon is where fingers measure transience. I turn to you to see if you are still alive. Holes of fog everywhere. I dare not touch you, for fear of waking you.

11

I want you to keep for yourself these words lulled from our last embrace. Hands, wet as mud, cannot speak. Outside, it is Sunday. Time for chimes and prayers. No image for anxiety which floats between heaven and earth. Music. Melody. Vegetation, when it deafens the city, emits noises too strident for the hurting eardrum. Grass stains. For our last bid, we bend on our knees and let the landscape impress itself on us: incredible relief of flesh.

12

You are asleep. I am alone in the garden. We expect no visitor. The day is slow in recounting its story. I bury my brain under the leaves near me, and wait. My head like a dead tree trunk, torn off; my eyelids completely useless. I can't hear a sound. Later, I'll make my way to you. I'll yawn to postpone fatigue, and whisper that love is a night we tear from bad dreams. Then I'll leave – my tongue's clink in your ear.

13

Or perhaps eyes will caress spaces and plants with names I don't know. Windows left open. Perhaps the bedsheet will blossom before May, your body be removed from time. Each single hour lifts the day higher, destroying my humble tasks one by one. A prism shatters in the sky, without dazzle. You awake as the light transforms angles into curves. You find me beside you, a book in my hands, my eyes hanging on to the colour blue, vertical, immobile.

14

All gardens are alike, all trees alike at sunset; parks, forests around cities, alike, the hardwood floors in rooms wherever we find ourselves, nights, night fatigue, the infinity of sleep during all the nights of all the summers, alike. Lying beside you, all I do is look at you. You are asleep. I'm on guard. A few more minutes to fight back the horror. Eyes veiled by a layer of thinning skin. Darkness so faithfully dark. Darkness starving. Can you see that I'm not the woman you think I am, I'm not the woman I am.

15

The day folds during the fall. Reading. The fingernails are bloody as we shut the lid of the casket. My nightgown rolled up to my groin like moss, I'm reading aloud. Reading. You raise your arms towards me. This is the beginning of another human epic. Aloud. We pull the names out of our throats tightened by weeping, and start to walk through the endless landscape which spreads its patterns before us. You rest at the window, effortlessly, the garden, the vegetation, the white side of the word *joy*. I'm reading.

A HOLE OF SILENCE

1993

1

What we hear in the moaning
of dreams is a call
appearance of a face
without features
angel or markings
pulling solitude
out of our deep mourning
no word comes to mind
for these everyday objects
no offering for these hungry gods
truth is a silence
asleep over our ears
silence is a hole
that swallows the night

2

Our tongue's forever surprised
by the countless dead
between our teeth
the gape hangs
like a drape
no one remembers
how to rock
the temple with a requiem
trembling
feverish
quiet
the pole roughly
northbound
we measure the sky
against the tenuity
of the day

3

Small struggles
small painful wounds
we dress sadness
with the tulle
torn off the wedding dress
we darken
page after
page
buried in our palms
which we lift to the splendours
of this century

a dim light
flickers in the murky waters
of our eyes

4

Our lips move
timidly
to the light
vivid colours
of the city coming to life
with people
perhaps we should recite
a prayer
for the way the day hangs
on to the night
in this never-ending
ebbing
of nights and days
what a mystery
to hear the echoes
of a familiar melody
drowning
then rising
above the world

5

They call it singing
this wail of mine rising
before this shroud
this dazed
man's opened mouth
closing on the vowels
of his name
on Sunday the sea
breaks against the temple
I wait for a sacrifice
truth pins
nothingness
onto the landscape
and all its perfection

6

We want a simple
crisis to tell
a mouth
slashed by a knife
misery and blood
in large circles
like a drawing on a pillow
it starts with the purple
of the funeral
one girl alone
alive in his eyes

extreme excuse
thrown against the world
extreme love

7

Each day moves
closer to our eyes
an unfamiliar stain
under the fading
flickering light
that turns into wings
or the whiteness
of a bird's feathers
hanging on the broken
frame of a painting
and then this question

how many colours
to hide
the thickness of tears

8

Viewed from above
the soul is a shadow
broken by an inhospitable
river and the small of morning
a wall
of light enclosing
the sky and eternity
heard in between calls
someone pulls us back to life
but the gods fall
quietly asleep
and are deaf
to the pitiful cries
of orphans

9

Too much memory
blinds the day
the large silhouette
sometimes quivers
in the felt of our eyes
where love lowers
painfully its weight
we speak of wear and tear
and straws and beams
why worry if we blink
in front of it all
just one heartbeat knocks over
the setting now freed of its surfaces
a bombshell explodes in our wombs

10

At vespers
horses fly away
and liberate the skies
at the end of the night
animals unfold their enormous
wings against the horizon
wider than our sight
this is another evening
another existence
another pair of eyes
down at the tip
of our lids and something white
cheats the gaping graveyard
of all its certainties

11

Once again
for one last time
the hour exhausts
the seriousness of its seconds
we will be ready for the wake
continents will shift
towards the oceans
between our lips
there, at the threshold
where the procession stops
where statues
of salt and saliva
gulp the black blood
stolen from the living

12

But death lasts for a second
space will one day escape us
and we will awake
with islands under our eyelids
overfed animals
will rock with the rumble
of the torrent
the heart will give birth
to the earth
and under the stare
of dazzled angels

one by one
constellations
will burn ablaze

WITHOUT A WITNESS

1997

I

You were a woman
of little details:
a ribbon, a wedding band
found in the sand,
laughter that resonated
before and after wars.
You sailed the seas
as black as your womb,
following the steps
of a crazy dance you danced
back when you believed you loved
the men you loved.
Today you are looking for a place
where your shadow will not fall prey
to nostalgia.

II

You have piled your cries
of love and hate
under an old lampshade,
as though you had to leave yourself
before touching hope
on your skin.
You want to learn how to say
words that follow the perfect beat
of sunlight,
such is your illusion, your naive happiness,
the kind you write about
in those poems
you polish late into the night
in your bedroom where you run to,
unaware how terrible
morning's revenge will be.

III

You love apple trees
when they are in full
bloom,
before their branches are weighed down
by fruit, before they are
plundered,
you love the wind
in the leaves
and how it blows into your blouse
revealing your breasts
to tranquillity.
You are not afraid to keep silent
and compose songs with landscapes
innocent of sadness.

Life, you say, is reality
you cannot clutch
with the fingers of a single hand.

IV

Night catches up to you,
leaving you shivering
in the early morning.
At times you find yourself dreaming,
eyes wide open,
fixed on the crypt you carry
within you, as you stroll
among slanted tombstones.
You no longer try to distinguish
sweat from deceased bodies,
the world converges into a subtle odour
that jolts the day awake
from the indifference of smell.
You never walk down
the same path twice.

V

You realize it,
when vespers chime,
all orchards look the same,
trees,
flowers, and the blueness of light
you carry on your shoulders,
as you step into the intimate writing
world scarcely
awakened.
You stand there, without a witness,
until it is time
to defer time.
You occupy your solitude
with the impertinence
of a cloudless sky.

VI

Yet you lack the arrogance
of July stars that flatten the night
against the fat countryside,
and these words, almost sacred,
which you will not let go,
except when silence
becomes more arrogant than you.
You hesitate to choose
between the earth and the verticality
of souls that haunt you
until the morning shines its light on you,
just as the world begins to move with life
in all its opacity.

A splinter sometimes
sticks into your finger –
this is one victory
daylight will claim for you.

SO CLOSE

1998

When the sky grows small I find myself nowhere, belonging to no forest or city, a woman feeling small in her womanhood, trying to catch sight of her reflection in a chance windowpane. There, remembering my own death, the precise moment I stopped breathing, I silently rock myself, glad to find myself intact in the willingness of the world, glad to offer my name up to the teeth of the sun. It is still day, even though the day has long set, I keep a watchful eye on the flowers in the cemetery. I keep vigil on myself, standing quiet among the souls that have succumbed.

Around me, too many crises I should have undone. Too much silence. As though stirring awake men and women from their misery, I risk surrendering to being devoured in public, my womb slit open, my insides eaten by starving beasts. Yet writing begins with the shame of one's own sordid death, always, one hand faltering, clinging to truth, freeing itself of childhood's body, the white opaqueness that envelopes memory.

Writing always begins with a betrayal.

We become the child we never were, insolent with insects buzzing around our heads. Something belonging to the world makes its way inside, we no longer wish to keep out, a purity of suffering. It sweeps through, pushing us off our bed, the night of great darkness where we do not expect beauty to appear, just the surprise of being able to move and feel our vocal chords about to burst. We say that we are broken voices above the rumbling, wanting to give life to the fossilized stone.

We can never really see the entire truth, truth as it appears to us when we are strolling along and the sky seems to hide behind the mountain. Just enough of truth that permits hope of dreams to fly free, a house, a wall covered with photographs and books, an angel that spreads its wings in light and love. Love minus the end of love, love without end that we attempt to stamp on to the sound of our foot-steps so as to make it all real, music that fills the city with a sense of relief, as though all its avenues lead to a sea fading with forgetfulness.

The poem, yes, we must all lose ourselves. The city is rumbling, always the same noise, a moaning that becomes insistent when we rest, our heads drunken with pictures as old as a life, good-bye, sadness, tiny disasters that turn us into scared animals running to a hidden creek to lick their wounds. The poem. The poem that awaits us when we at last surrender, the stuttering that happy men and women emit when they rise from hell.

Once again I would like to believe that night begins with a simple gesture, a hand stretching out to another hand, without a wedding band, in the summer, insects dancing all around. I would like to believe that night is night, when forgiveness is joyous, almost a face, with enough forgetfulness to make us mistake surrendering for happiness, fear for prayer. It is not unusual for me to say we when it is I who succumbs to seduction, as if love were secretly bound to the deceptions of the skin.

In the evening I slip into the disheveled hair of the garden, the light from lamps on the willows, the air lazily caressing the stones, everything is about to fall sound asleep, children, birds in fairy tales and their singing louder than images. I dream about love so that summer remains between my legs. I say *utopia* when I mean *freedom*, such is the patience required to pull melancholy, hidden words riddled with despair I so strongly want to believe in, for as long as my dust is dust.

No doubt, when I was a child, some tried hard to make me forget that I would die, no doubt. All I need is to free myself of time for the world to stop turning. I dig my rooks deep in the ideas of books illuminated with sand and gold, where we see what lies behind eyes, behind fear and distant failures. I notice how the rough ends up in the words of a poem.

The poem, yes, I survive each one of my deaths.

NOTES ON SURVIVAL

2002

To J.P.

First Note

One morning you sat down to write. It was summer, during the hottest period of the summer, and like in a postcard, it was sunny, sweat everywhere, life in full swing, love in the air. You sat down that morning, laptop on your thighs. Call it summer writing, the sort of writing that brings life melting with heat to a halt, so you can appreciate the vine hanging on the window, its fruits ready to be plucked. In spite of the world gone wrong, writing was brimming with hope. Not lightness. Hope. Gentleness. You came to understand how *lightness* and *hope* shared little in common. That morning you could not judge the weight of those two terms. You were busy stringing sentence after sentence that a woman had written. Later, in the afternoon, you heard the one you love pronounce the word *illness,* and right then fiction faded and was replaced by reality. You wept, wondering if the words of a poem or a novel could ever replace the arms stretching out to you. You asked yourself the question half-heartedly, without serious intent. When there is suffering, one word matters: survival. You tossed the literary stuff aside and consulted a dictionary on medicine.

Second Note

Medicine says nothing about how cells sometimes go wrong. Not a word about the anguish that easily crams the room when words prove useless. Not a word about the vulnerability you feel when you notice the drop before you. Not a word about how desire grabs you in the morning when you least expect it. Not a word about the nervous laughter stronger than any diagnosis. Not a word about the future. All mouths seem busy conjugating verbs in all tenses. Nothing about how time is sometimes stubborn. Not a word about the trust pulling you up onto your feet when you don't want to rise. Not a word about the relief you find the moment you notice life no longer feels the same. Not a word about the beauty of time-present, the two of you sitting, at sunset, sipping a glass of wine. Not a word about the love that summons strength, or the strength that summons life.

Doctors know best. Thanks.

Third Note

Poetry starts when the language of science ends, when science admits defeat for failing to encompass the magnitude of reality. Poetry notices the fault and starts digging a breach, an opening where normal syntax is powerless. This presence in the world makes you question what took many years to learn, things that those around you kept repeating, that this was the only possible way, to smother under the burden of words. The moment you stop being the obedient student is when poetry appears. When you say, *I see things differently.* When you are able to say *I.*

Poetry starts when you free yourself of religious, family, political, scientific and literary dogmas. Poetry takes many paths at once, encouraging you to doubt, question, resist, revolt, subvert. Poetry forces you to sit, face to face, with the past. Poetry inspires distancing, renunciation, destruction. What others might call *negativity.*

You prefer the term *destruction.* It's radical. More violent. Which entitles you to fight disease with disease. A practice western medicine does not endorse.

Fourth Note

Taking the pose of a fighter, you're ready to face reality. This struggle is unlike anything you have had in the past, fighting, for instance, for social justice. Nevertheless, that is where you learned the basics of all struggles. This new challenge requires that you use all you have learned to achieve survival. The means: action, words, texts.

Action. You and the man you love will not change. You will cook a meal for friends, you will watch TV, you will go for the daily walk. You look forward to coming Sunday and talk at length about a painting you both like. You will live each moment fully, conscious now of how important the present moment is. Something that you never did before.

Words. You will mention the illness, so as to contain it, but you will forbid it to pervade the space you share together. At times, yes, the illness will appear before you like a mountain, but like on a trip it will vanish in the distant haze. Illness is not something one forgets easily. You want to push it into the background, like a half-formed idea, far from the light of day.

Texts. No word for a poem comes to mind. The present tense of poetry has smashed into the stronger wall of reality. You need to think about it for a while, keeping things in perspective. You weave these notes in a notebook not because writing can heal – you're not that foolish, you want something to spark new energy. You hear whispered a slogan people used to say: *Victory is ours.*

This notebook is for him, as though he were writing it together with you. You should use the plural here. It just occurs to you what the word *dedication* means.

Fifth Note

Sunny again today. The grapes ripen under the window. Birds. The perfect postcard one finds in a bad poem. No matter what bad poetry you have read, you're still under the spell of this world. Offered to you alone. You wonder how you will filter light through the poem, the shadows on the brick wall, the various tinges of green in leaves, the squabbling of birds. How will you mix poetry and life ignorant of the whining found in so many books?

What makes a poem good? Vision? Imagination? The mastery of language? An awareness of tradition? The ability to innovate? All of the above, you have repeated that so often in your creative writing workshops. Still, there is a question you have not dared ask yourself, surely never in those creative classes: what distinguishes a good poem from a great poem, the poem that leads you to territories you did not know existed? Perhaps, it is the quality of the relationship the writer establishes between himself and the world, a relationship that demands from the writer being in its totality.

Being in its totality. The brain alive with thoughts, contradicting itself, being imaginative. The heart, the seat of love, but also restlessness, distress, anger, yes, anger too. Sex and the hunger for life. The senses, all five senses, not only those that work at a distance: sight and hearing, but the primary senses as well: touch, taste, smell. Five senses, and a sixth one too: the one positivists banished and which we have come to call, for lack of a better term, *intuition*. This is the sense, though no science will back you on this, that pushes you to say to the man you love that he will live forever.

The poet's wager: to come as close as possible to the world and let it cut a path through language. Not *in* language, *through* language. With more or less successful coincidences. Approximations.

Sixth Note

You started to speak like you used to, without thinking. You amend some poems. There are no minor and major poems. In the large poetry anthologies we find two sorts of poems: essential poems and the other kind, those that, according to you, do not establish a particular meaning of truth towards reality. They procrastinate in literature. Finely wrought poems, often brilliant, but distilled by lukewarmness, moderation, propriety of the times. Commonness. Craftsmanship. Lacking in originality.

The moment you understand the true meaning of *illness*, you no longer care for literature that poses as literature. Your guts no longer care for such pretense. Nor do you subscribe to any respectable idea of what poetry is supposed to be. For example, writing changes the course of things. Affirmations of this sort may comfort the poet who needs to feel useful, they nourish the illusions that he is not wasting his time. But such concepts leave you cold.

What transforms one's existence is the panoply of New Year's resolutions: love, money, health, or, if these are impossible, an able doctor and effective drugs and cures.

Poetry speaks what is not spoken, expresses beauty, joy, anger, pain, revolt.

Seventh Note

When you asked the man you love if he felt like screaming, he replied, No. Nor did you feel like screaming. That would have been a waste of time, what time is left you want to dedicate to fighting. Fighting for survival. The dictionary defines *survival* as the state of surviving someone; life after death; the fact of surviving, staying alive. In each case, survival is something that seems to come *after:* after someone; after death; after health.

What concerns you is what happens in the end. Does staying alive necessarily mean that one is living? No. Paradoxically, when we think of survival, life resonates with the unheard of significance. The grapes on the vine, the glass of wine on the table, the nervous laughing at something stupid, all the while anxiety stuck like a bone in your throat. What is futile becomes necessity. The more insignificant an image is the more meaningful it becomes. Like a poem.

True poetry is what connects you to life, especially when you know that life will come to an end. Every single word in a poem activates a heart beat, pumping blood into your veins. If poetry does not have the power to heal, it can at least kindle a flame, the fire that motivates the reader to stand up for a fight.

To fight. Admire how the grapes have matured on the vine. Listen to what you could not hear yesterday. Crickets, the meowing of the cat in the alley, the silence of a sleepless night. *To fight.* The greatest battles are the small ones, those that we wage against the absurdities of existence. As weapons all you possess are your eyes and ears and hands. A poem can be of service here, reminding you of the gifts you forgot you have.

Eighth Note

"Your bones have not been affected." You listened, tough as stone, to the hospital doctor explaining the results of the examination. You stared at his hand on the phone, at the pencil in the other hand, and listened to his voice repeating the file number. When the doctor hung up, he gave you the verdict: "Your bones have not been affected." You grabbed the wrist of the man you love and pressed your lips to his fingers. You had just heard one of the most beautiful sentences in the world.

"Your bones have not been affected." Six words, the last being multi-syllablic. Can such a sentence ever make it as a verse in a poem? You could turn the phrase into a metaphor, but it would lack the impact it had in real life. The beautiful lines you hear in real life rarely become verses.

You know that poets are lying to you when they praise the power of poetry. Poetry is like natural medicine: it helps only those whose existence is not endangered. If you are standing on a scaffold or in front of a doctor hanging onto a phone, poetry is of no use.

Ninth Note

A simple sentence like "Your bones have not been affected" got the motor turning again. Time unfolded like a landscape and uprooted the word *future* from the obsession of time-present. Poetic vertigo does not arise from a sound, a syllable or a word ready to topple an entire verse. Nor is it heedless prose waiting to gush out. Poetry is the result of tension between the continuity of a sentence and the verticality of a verse. A requirement for poetry in prose. The fight must go on.

The moment you become aware that you have to fight to survive, poetry dwindles in the background. The state of survival paradoxically throws you right into poetic time. This is not a contradiction. Life takes the place of a poem, life turns into poetry. Is this the reason why you are incapable of writing poetry these days? Nothing comes when being is "the general unsettling of the senses" (Rimbaud). Let poetry come after, when living is easy. The urge to stir a little chaos into language will come back to you. Days will then be chapters of a story without history. A glass of wine will hold no greater significance than it should. Only then will you be able to write a poem again.

Tenth Note

Poetry can never replace reality. This much, poets have admitted. Poetry becomes meaningful after life settles down and regains peace. Yet poetry needs to come into contact with the real world, keeping it alive, regardless of time. Whenever a poet commits a line to a piece of paper, for himself and others, you feel the joy of creation, because there occurs unexpectedly the necessary bridging with the world: a crazy belief in eternity. You have one wish: that death not be the last word.

What remains of the poetic gesture is the power of the gesture itself. Yves Bonnefoy writes: "*For the time being* we will have grown old. The word as action develops in the same lapse of time as any action." The man you love will soon be healthy. Soon you will be counting time in decades, instead of minutes.

The poems you wrote in summer will read as though written by a stranger. One day, you will have to write about that particular summer, for you know that illness will never disappear, and that others who suffer like the man you love will need to read poems. You will be writing again. It is a good thing to take your time with poems. Is it you who wants to continue living? That your hands might, indeed, be useless does not make living easy.

Eleventh Note

Before reality stands a poet whose hands are rough and soft. He has wounds, scars, new wrinkles that appear with the passing of time. His nails are dirty, his fingers move slowly, stretching out to a stranger. But he knows that this stranger might not want to shake his hand, might not feel the need to bridge two lives. Still, the poet is no different than his "soul brother" (Rutebeuf); he too wants to be accepted by the world. If he wants to write, he must first rid himself of clichés and stereotypes.

Writing. To be as close as possible to feelings, emotions, impressions, ideas of time-present, even if you're scared of not being able to capture the true colour of the vine. Describe how the vine is a hand caressing the window. That's a fair start.

Every time you draw a line, it is as if the entire world were behind you. As if. Let's face it: you're unable to live outside the world you have created parallel to the real one. This is the closest you'll ever get to having faith, even though you don't believe in an afterlife.

You're not alone with this need of faith.

Twelfth Note

After telling the man you love the good news, the doctor asked: "Do you want to live?" He didn't hesitate and answered, Yes. And you, too, want him alive. To watch him live, you must yourself be alive. Absolutely.

"Do you want to live?" A question you often find in books. It's the basis. And poetry screams Yes to the world. Yes to yourself, as you sit writing, a laptop on your thighs.

Printed in November 2005
at Gauvin Press Ltd., Gatineau, Québec